Finding Pahaquarra

poems by

D. Scott Humphries

Finishing Line Press
Georgetown, Kentucky

Finding Pahaquarra

for Amy

Copyright © 2020 by D. Scott Humphries
ISBN 978-1-64662-196-5 First Edition
All rights reserved under International and Pan-American Copyright Conventions. No part of this book may be reproduced in any manner whatsoever without written permission from the publisher, except in the case of brief quotations embodied in critical articles and reviews.

ACKNOWLEDGMENTS

Grateful acknowledgment is made to the editors of the following publications, in which some of the poems in this collection first appeared (often in earlier form):

Community College Moment, Sancturary: Portage (The Journey North), Refugee, Is home
Exit 13 Magazine, Number 24: Chick Severe's Garden, Visiting My Godson
Exit 13 Magazine, Number 25 (forthcoming): Motorheads
Sensations Magazine Supplement 8, Westward Expansion: Moving: Language of Trade, 1784
This Broken Shore, Vol XII No. 1: Murph Jones' Secret

"Motorheads" has been nominated for a 2019 Pushcart Prize.

Publisher: Leah Maines
Editor: Christen Kincaid
Cover Art: *Mount Tammany* by Ricky of Luna Parc, www.lunaparc.com
Author Photo: Richard Boscarino
Cover Design: Elizabeth Maines McCleavy

Printed in the USA on acid-free paper.
Order online: www.finishinglinepress.com
also available on amazon.com

Author inquiries and mail orders:
Finishing Line Press
P. O. Box 1626
Georgetown, Kentucky 40324
U. S. A.

Table of Contents

Portage (The Journey North) 1

Moving: Language of Trade, 1784 2

Rafting 3

Come tramping with me 5

Chick Severe's Garden 7

Refugees 8

Sandy's Song 9

Murph Jones' Secret 11

Hugh, of Donegal 12

Listening to Trees 13

Motorheads 14

Finding Pahaquarra 16

Saving Sunfish Pond 18

Robert Plant's Hair 19

Goof takes us to Pahaquarra 21

The Color of Christmas 23

Goof does Driver's Ed 24

Fire at Foul Rift 25

Coconut Oil 26

In the Kitchen 27

Visiting My Godson 28

Stillwater Summer 29

Birdie 30

Is home 32

Portage (The Journey North)

My dream so troubling, I have had to burn cedar,
to call up my mother wrapped in fur, a pelt
joined to her hair. In her arms, I was calmed.
She spoke the old legend, how the animals left
Lenape'hokink, Land of Lenape, went north
to where the spruce grows. They returned to us only
when we learned to respect their full being
in life and in death, to take only what's needed
and to honor them and the land.

This we taught to the first Wapsitak—a Swede married
my sister—but now come the English, who pay us no mind
other than to deceive us, to trick us and conquer those
who would teach them how to hold the animals here.
The sons of our friend, William Penn, and their agent, ran
man ahead on a deal to mark borders by walking, then
taking the grounds of the Munsee from the river, inland.
I must move again.

I have pushed north to where water ends,
where Lenapewihhituk begins, I can paddle
no further, my arms must now carry my vessel on land,
as I go north to the spruce where the animals hid.
I am tired of killing, I am tired of death, nothing
around me is left of all that I've known.
Where we came to so long ago is now the place
we come from; it is taken and changed.
I dreamt of faraway places said once to be our homeland,
land bridges and journeys hundreds of ancestors ago.

Lenape'hokink is all that I've known but for now
I must leave it, like the otter and beaver, until we live
again, here, where the sons of the English will one day
know that my people are truly their fathers, their mothers,
their sisters, their brothers, their kin.

We shall all come again.

Moving: Language of Trade, 1784

On the Delaware, moving, November.
Gliding in dugout, I do not use
your words for land, water or time.
I will not utter those sounds for you
in my mother's tongue—you
need only my language of trade, expressions
for corn, or knives, beads and cloth.
I bid you fair commerce,
yet you want discussion,
persuasion for your god, polemic
of politic, systems not native.
If you come to barter, I will meet you
with beaver skins, thinner than a northern pelt,
still as soft. If you come to settle,
I will find you, turn you out.
I do not own this land—
I belong to it. You are here
by directive, under instruction. I allow,
never sell. Your documents I disclaim,
merely nod; your discourse contains you.
As the river freezes, I move freely upon it.
You are forced into forts, still ships
in harbor. I will meet you,
share my language of trade.
Or I will find you,
share my message of death.
I am peaceful but I am not weak.
I protect my people.
We remain many, despite your disease.
The Susquehannock know this. You shall
know it as well. I give you my vow.
Your writing is worthless,
your promises empty.
You will take without asking.
I will answer in time.

Rafting

I

Soft day in a summer of days trying hard
to impress or at least be less bored,
Goof made a decision that we'd tube
the Pequest from the school at White Township
straight on through to the river.

I'd tubed in circles at the Lake, stroked
canoes out on the streams, water no stranger,
besides, we had beer. Except for the culvert
just beyond Island Park, that day
nowhere near us, we sailed safe through

cow pastures on Pequest Drive, so shallow
in some spots we had to get out and wade,
to the deep lazy bend at the old A&P,
six packs cooling and dragging us slower,
sultry and sun-filled, we slurried to town.

We pulled out at the millrace, in a still quiet
eddy, up from two sets of falls and the
final steep rapids. I was sure I heard
rushing, even felt icy spray. Goof said
it took longer than ever, or we'd have

made it down to the Delaware and gone
farther south. The rest of us whispered all
puzzled and beer thick, he can't mean we'd tube
Foul Rift, we'd all heard the stories, Goof was
out of his mind. Then, finally out of

the water, we were dry, out of danger.
We trudged back to the barn.

II

Winter they cleared trees closest to banks,
close to the water, threw them on eddy ice,
waiting for spring thaw, then

lashed them together into large rafts on the river
until the high freshets took them over Foul Rift
to Trenton Falls into Philly, to the lumber mills

there, then on into the shipyards. Ironmen steering,
or falling, or drowning, or ducking at every low
covered bridge. Easton was tricky, but offered

good food and lodging, grand entertainment, belles,
board and beer. These were the trees and the rafters
who steered them, later turned into lumber that

crafted the ships of the nation, the homes of the
Valley where the settlers would live until the late
1900s, when dam water threatened,

not the sky, not the thaw, not the high running river
or the current that drew them, or their cargo,
south into progress at the dawn of an age.

Come tramping with me

All you need carry is clothes
and not many, come
tramping with me. Sounds
fine but it ain't. It's romantic
as dirt and that's how they'll treat you,
the other bums, not the public,
most people ignore you, won't
even see you, you'll end up like me.
You may come out fine
but you'll always be hungry,
all night, all day till a hint
of mowed grass on the wind
makes you drool and your stomach
flip over. You'll give up your
real name, be called Professor
or Utah. You're young, agile, good
looking, you'll need my protection.
I never knew drifters could use boys
like women, something I know now—
hold them down, choke them blind
into submission, take whatever life's
left. You'll need my assistance
if you ride on the rails, boxcars
clicking like bugs in your mind,
always there scheming, two steps
behind desperation. You might as well
try it, there's nothing to lose like a real job
since you've lost that already
and won't find another, you'll get
food on the fly, maybe circus work,
road work, fleas or worse in your kit,
you know what that's like, you've
already been bit by Wall Street creepos
and cheapos who fracture your life,
rob your money, take even your wife.

Forget it all, tramp with me, now and then
we'll find water to drink or to bathe in,
you'll only be grimy if you let yourself
go. I'm headed west to the desert,
they're building a dam there, and the WPA's
felling trees in the Rockies, I hope
I'll find work there or a handout
or two. It's no longer a choice, son,
just all I can do.

Chick Severe's Garden

Riding atop my father's shoulders, after a June Jersey rain,
my sister had the best view of Chick Severe's garden
as he strutted, puffed and smiled us through a tour
on his large lot in Allamuchy, early evening,
singsong crickets the only music, far from
the house, way back by the property line and forest.

Remember, my sister said, how we went back
a year or two later and Route 80, freshly laid asphalt,
newly granted access, 3,000 miles direct to San Francisco,
cut right through the carrot patch. By then Chick was grayer,
stooped, his mouth set even. Deaf to the traffic as well as
the crickets, on that visit he shook his head
side to side and didn't say much, pointed at the roadway
with rheumy eyes, toured us this time to tell the tragic tale
or to say good bye. He died

shortly after, gray to white to dust. His wife Angie
sold the house before the first thud of Delaware Valley dirt
hit the coffin lid, but not to the government—never
to the government. They'd done enough damage, taken
enough homes already, it turns out for nothing

more than a handful of tears and a box full of bones. Just
northwest of Chick's land there's a national park
where there was almost a man-made lake and dammed river,
hiker's visit now—natural trails remain—but the folk
drowned out anyway, houses mulched or discarded,
bone to ash, ash to air, air to ghosts

in the gardens, up the trees, rustling leaves,
the woods still standing, the only wood left standing.

Refugees

Returning from fourteen years abroad,
a teacher, not a soldier, not that era
anyway, when returning military,
maligned, turned to drug and drink,
still, I feel a refugee in the land of my birth,
the state of my youth. Quiet
in heart of forest, endless pine and birch,
oak nearly bald now in the bright November sun—
streams clean enough to drink, clear enough
to see red, brown, black pebbles magnified
to sparkle, but among people awkward,
frightened, unsure of what to say
or how to say it, supposing
I'd been more articulate living in lands
where I didn't speak or hold the tongue—
I still knew how to see a soul and touch it.
Is this how they felt forced out of their homes
back when the dam loomed large,
groundbreaking due any day, then forgotten
as others moved in to build communes
and communities on the fragile wind—
who is stranger when you stand
one town over and up the mountain watching
the Valley change, buildings buried or burned,
history razed. I have returned to renewed,
abandoned land. I stay but I am skittish.
When I feel unsure, I drive to find peace
at Pahaquarra, aware that some still cannot cross
the border into the Park without breaking down
on the shoulder of Old Mine Road.

Sandy's Song

I will speak with you only
so it may never happen again
here or anywhere
else. It's a painful past chapter
from a water-stained book,
took a long time to close.
Now, here you are asking,
picking at scars.

I will speak to you bitter
sweet, so that the stories
are told and remembered,
those who died early,
their souls shoved aside,
fostering cancer, or illness
after losing their land
that the government owns
without owning
up to what they have taken.

I see the Park Service
inflating the numbers:
seven thousand cars daily
commute Dingmans Bridge.
I will not trust them
even if they turn traffic
clear out of Layton
and lease back the land.
Vision 2030 remains
to be seen. Hold them
accountable, honor my time:

I speak to your poetry,
each story a breeze
or a rustle on wind
of someone who's walked
these trees at least some time,
at least one time,
before being moved on
or moving, I will speak
to you now.

Murph Jones' Secret
for Norma Bernstock

September 1904, Murph jumped sixty-five feet off
the span of the new Belvidere Bridge, plunged
into the Delaware, popped up like a burnt cork.

People palmed their eyes watching, paid their money
to coax him, or pay for his coffin after the dive, but Murph
survived, collected ten dollars—more than a week's pay

as the town's best black trash boy—got so greased by midnight
you couldn't tell him apart from the dark,
but for wild eyes. Murph had a secret, he knew the Pequest

raging down to the Delaware, had carved
a deep hole there, on the south Jersey side,
right under the bridge, secret nursed all summer

as the new tall steel structure went up to replace
the low wooden bridge, lost in the Pumpkin Flood
last October, a secret that saved him from slurs,

proud secret, a talisman, kept his head tall mornings
stepping over the gutters where he'd passed out
and pissed himself the evening before. Murph brought

that secret back every September, dropped into the shallows,
Jersey side of the river, summer-low for the season,
the crowd gasped and cheered. Smile as white

as the docile flock he fleeced, he always
dove in a drunk, emerged an entrepreneur,
early days, a new century, progress as full

as Murph's pocket of change.

Hugh, of Donegal

Out of streaming river bank fog
in emerald-green hoody you rose,
rust-red hair, freckle scars, war-whoops
falling to laughter, we played.

Directly on the Delaware's edge,
fingers slipping, polished rocks,
I heard the harp,
penny whistle—
the ballad's trill—
or the robin's dawn song.
You raised a cry, set upon me
dancing.

I've no longer any idea of your name.
You must be Hugh, of Donegal,
after your brilliant, fire-some hair, like the boy
in the film, Wonderful World of Walt Disney.

You had escaped the tower. Together,
we had reached boats that would save us away.

Listening to Trees

The trees are talking together,
my father said when
October winds bent branches low,
forcing leaves to the ground.
He raked bright yellow-red piles we jumped
in and out of. He never asked us to help,
only whistled along.

Weekends my father burst into our bedrooms,
jolly wake up time singing, stereo blaring:
*seventy-six trombones caught the morning sun
with one hundred and ten cornets close at hand.*
After church, Mulligans in Oxford for the paper
and three pieces of candy. Then we'd go
to the Water Gap. You could say we grew up there.

Looking up, dad convinced us the face of a chieftain
jutted out from the slate of Mount Tammany,
looking just right you'd see it,
carved by rain out of sandstone and granite,
or mysteriously by the Lenape to remember
their leader. My dad wasn't a dreamer
but Sundays were legend. On the way home,
magical places along Route 46—Hunter's Lodge,
King Cole's Grove, and then Hot Dog Johnny's.

I never learned to rake leaves,
but I learned how to listen
to maples and birches and the tales
they can tell. I'm hopeless at yardwork
yet I see Native features in the hills
while out hiking, humming the music
of a grand marching band.

Motorheads

He moved the wiper knob on the hood of his Datsun,
sprayed me each time I biked past.
When I finally stopped, he explained the mechanics
without starting the car, his only interest.
He was eighteen so he made it sound cool.
He said he'd been drafted, this his last weekend
before heading to 'Nam,
spent at his aunt's place up at the lake,
just that, nothing more.
Nothing about burning his draft card, hitchhiking to Canada
like some kids at college, like I thought I'd have to
someday. Nothing about guns with live ammo or
the taste of metal in a mouth so dry
he couldn't even smile that day on that road
in front of that cottage. Nothing about what
swarmed like July lightening bugs above my bike
and his ride.

I should have asked, maybe. I considered myself
worldly. I read all kinds of books, knew about
all kinds of things without knowing at all
how heavy the war was, the news in full color
on the three nightly networks in my peripheral vision,
my parents all worried, older kids right out of high school
ripped from home to bleed out in some rice field,
alone and away. No one really knew why, or how long
it would last or if we were next.

I should have asked for his overseas address,
could've written daily about my bike and the beach,
swimming out to the raft, about summer rains
at the lake, on the Delaware River, flooding the cornfields
seeping into my plans. I'd ask about weather,
the monsoon on the Mekong, about which I'd read.

He poked my arm before I started to cry.
Hey, will you take my wheels? Not to keep,
but to hold until I return. You don't have to worry
if you're too young to drive, just keep her safe
in the garage, out of sight.

Finding Pahaquarra

Everything I knew of Pahaquarra
flowed past the footpath under the bridge—
a slab of concrete set into the creek
in the tunnel beneath Old Mine Road.

Everything I knew of Pahaquarra
drove up there with me and my dad
in Chick Severe's turquoise Ford
full of men smoking, cussing,

burning my eyes. Everything,
I knew of Pahaquarra sold at the
trading post—first time I tasted
popsicles called strawberry shortcake

and chocolate eclair. Everyone,
assembled on the parade field,
swimming, boating the river, headed
out to an island we never could reach

and weren't sanctioned to visit.
Bunkhouses of boys surprisingly
unsupervised. Perfecting my racing
dive, weaving a basket, hiking

a trail, pissing into the dirt, never
showering alone. Up early, mess duty,
gray-green stiff oatmeal; an archery range,
a hundred strung bows, a thousand

silver-tipped arrows. Loose red
flannel shirts; campfire smoke clung
to my clothes, hung there weeks after.
Everything I knew of Pahaquarra

now missing on drives there, a few
ruined foundations, no longer a trail in the
stream, though one day last autumn
I found remains of a stair in the bank,

a whiff of dad's old whisky pipe
smoke, as I portaged the bridge.

Saving Sunfish Pond

Another place I have walked past
with other boys while out hiking,
we did not stop to swim.
Brush, rather than beach,
reached to clear water, sharp rocks
beneath—or did we bare our feet
to take a few blistered miles
off the walking that day? We were
the only ones there, Sunfish Pond,
secret at the top of the trail.

I saw it more on the news, really,
or on stickers on the back of our cars.
Many made treks there, often in rain, with
day packs on their backs, media cameras,
justice supreme. "Save Sunfish Pond"
from becoming engulfed as part of a
larger planned lake, part of the pump station
already nearby. Instead, Sunfish Pond
became sacred, alone at the top of the trail.

We went on a field trip only once
to Yards Creek, took elevators down
into the guts of machinery, industrial
tan and green. Above us, humming and
clanging, buzzers, flashing red lights.
Back outside, we were gulping for air.

I think the Delaware perhaps saved itself,
but the people surely saved Sunfish Pond.
When Pahaquarra was moved away
from the river, over the mountain
to land at Yards Creek, timber rattlers,
greatly disturbed, attacked for awhile
before following the pipeline away
from the newly made campground
at the top of the trail.

Robert Plant's Hair

When I was an errant knight of sixteen,
I parted my shoulder length hair in the center,
like Robert Plant, like all sophomore boys
at my rural high school, like all the girls—
Sue and Val both begged to braid it,
tight overnight in order to kink it,
like everyone, I wanted to try it.
They came by just before supper,
wound tight my tresses. I pulled on
a ski-cap, armor against father
at head of the table, lord of the castle.
I approached knowing I'd cause
a commotion. He yelled
take off that cap. I gladly complied.
He screamed *put that damn hat
back on your damn head.*
I did so, smirking, expecting a lecture,
to hear condemnation of shoulder length hair
parted straight down the middle,
like Robert Plant. He finally looked up,
raised his glass for a toast,
wished me one day to have children
who behaved just like me.
The smirk tilted from me, my father, my better,
had just won the battle but not the campaign.
Next morning, braids out, head frizzed full, fluffed,
fantastic, I held court in the lunch room,
with Robert Plant's hair, my tale of rebellion,
and a way to fit in. I knew what to do,
in my way, to be cool.

Now I am an errant old knight, sixty-one,
and Robert Plant's hair has grown thin.
I never had kids who behaved just like me,
I never had children at all.
Sometimes I say, in the voice of my father—
as if he were standing right here—
put that damn hair
back on my damn head,
raising a toast of my own.

Goof takes us to Pahaquarra

We called him Goof, our alpha-omega,
no one could leave before he did.

When he hiked, he caught copperheads,
upside-down climbed rock faces,
never with harness, hard boots, or axe.

He commanded I drive us, deep winter,
to the ruins at Pahaquarra. He'd heard
the ice floes jammed high on the shore there,
tall crystal hallways he itched to explore.

We crunched across snow-pack, puffed Marlboro
vapor, trudged over the rise down to the bank.

Goof spun, wind whipped his down jacket,
looked right into my eyes and called me a pussy.

He thought I would not venture
out through icy stalagmites,
tall as tree towers, open, closing and drifting,
alive above water, moaning with wind-song.

Thought I would not dance with the rushes of winter,
said I would cop out. I would not walk on the water.

But I wanted to be first,
trusted the river to hold me.
It had once before, ten summers ago,
on this very spot—
the only one out of twenty, that year, to earn merit swimming.

I knew warm sands lurked below current season,
knew water moved surely; thus, so did I.

I ran out laughing. No one died as they followed,
though they trembled frostbitten.
We skated the ice floe, returned safely to shore.

Back at my car, Goof nodded, yet cursed me,
seemed shorter somehow. Sparking ignition,
in time with my breathing, I had driven us here.
I would now drive us home.

The Color of Christmas

The year he shaved his head and looked like a Nazi,
I saw the triangular scar I had caused there, when my brother
was eight and I twice his age. His winter-deep
blood on the heavy white snow, on the ice, at the Lake,
the color of Christmas, spreading, as he lay flat on his back.

The ice so perfect you could see two feet through it, ready
for skating. Overnight it had snowed a full foot upon it.
We set out to our beach to clear a small place, for my brother
for hockey, for my sister for playing, that morning
I shoveled in earnest, digging, lifting and tossing, straining

my arms until he got in my way, running, darting and yelling,
making faces I thought would look better under a shower
of snow. I threw a large shovel full at him and I meant it
to hurt him—I meant it to sting. With timing so awfully perfect,
he crossed right as I tossed, the corner caught his skull

ringing, he went down like a shot deer, blood started to flow.
My sister went screaming. I gathered him, running—
forty-eight steps up to the porch door—mom opened it wide-eyed
thought she heard *hit by a snowmobile*, her secret fear
every winter as they crisscrossed the lake, engines whining,

no, I said, crying, snow shovel, not snow mobile, let's get in the car.
Fifteen frantic miles to the doctor, on my lap on the backseat,
me holding his hand. Don't feel bad, they told me, after he
was all stitched up and dopey, accidents happen, you're not to blame.
Seeing the scar made the wound fresh again. I touched it

and told him I'd thrown snow on purpose at his face on that day.
I always knew, he said, *but, hey, I asked for it. Besides
the best part in the backseat was when you whispered to me
to squeeze fingers back to make sure I was breathing.
You grasped every five seconds. I hugged your hand right in return.*

Goof Does Driver's Ed

No matter how hard he tried, Goof could
never be older than me by a year.
It drove him crazy when I first got my license.
I loved that it bugged him, but never let on.
In my senior year, his junior year,
we ended up in a Chevy together,
3 p.m. Tuesdays, with Mr. Smith,
ex-marine, gym teacher, driving instructor.
He really scared me but I never let on.
I'd signed up to reduce the cost of insurance,
after getting my license, a very smart move.
So I drove us out from the High School and down
Foul Rift Road, did a K-turn and parked, then
got into the back seat, let Goof get up front.
I let them have the next hour together—
Goof learned to drive and I listened to tunes
on the radio Mr. Smith left playing ...
how long has this been going on,
loving you is easy cause you're beautiful,
you're the poetry man, third rate romance
low-rent rendezvous. If Tom Smith
surprised me, with his patience and kindness,
so unlike him yelling in gym class, then Goof
simply amazed me by taking direction,
nodding and listening, never once sneering.
Those May afternoons,
the bees, Bee Gees, warm breezes,
me snoozing the music, *loving you*
poetry man you're beautiful
ah, ah, ah, ah, staying alive.

Fire at Foul Rift

The alarm always startled. You'd hear it up Paul Street,
haunted wail without warning crying down Oxford Street,
squad up and out in a hurry if we were in class, but

I hadn't heard it, camping that Sunday out at the barn.
News came down later: fire had melted the trailer, charred
the fatally burned bodies but only one side.

The hour we all stumbled weed-heavy to bed, as we
slowly crashed, Allan had heard and had rushed out.
Allan who dabbled, until he found something better,

short blue-eyed bullshitter, every day except that one.
He came back in shock. We wandered up Race Street
in aimless short circles. I winced at his hoarse descriptions

of Rich, almost his brother, Tina, who'd been like a sister,
their baby, his godchild, and Karen, our friends. Lives we knew
that day burnt out on Foul Rift, close to the river,

flowing forcefully, cold and useless, nearby.
The fire raged itself out before the first truck arrived.

Coconut Oil

Some wore coconut oil instead of patchouli
for sale at the same head shop in Easton's
rough city center. In the back by the black lights,
the strobe lights and posters, in hard paper boxes
beyond brown wooden pipes, green plastic bongs,
Bambu rolling papers.

                                    Especially Cindy,
her long greasy straight hair, one lazy eye—
her bad reputation always hinting of summer.
She suffered no fools, bucked the administration,
we shared in-school suspension, caught smoking on grounds.

She'd wink with the good eye, say *keep on truckin'*,
liked being a waitress, loved being alive.

She'd pull out her dark vial, anoint our palms slowly,
rub liquid deep into our wrists while we dreamt of outrigging
on to islands and beaches.

Now you can get it at Shop Rite in a respectable aisle,
supposedly better for cooking than olive or others,
keeps your lipids in languor, coconut oil.

Everything sacred at some point renews,
shape shifts, solidifies, alters its power,
changes association, strengthens its base.

But on dark winter mornings
I still think only of Cindy,
while at the cast-iron skillet, conjuring eggs,
with that one lazy eye.

In the Kitchen

I can cook in the dark, all within reach,
pots, pans glittering, tinkling, late October
breezes, near time for holiday baking
as if it were the late 1970s—

mother and Charlotte, from two doors down,
in the breakfast nook conspiring
over cups of percolated coffee,
Gran drying dishes, returning them

to the wrong cupboards, the men yelling
at the TV, watching Joe Namath throw,
Special K cookies I'd made, chips and mom's
famous clam dip, dad's strawberry punch,

the aunts coming over, paying no mind
to me mixing my batter there in the kitchen,
listening as they dish out the roast,
the family dirt and regret, ghosts in the porcelain,

placemats set in December, gone by the
first, all within reach. I cook in the dark,
pots, pans tinkling, October glistening,
I can see in the dark, they are all within reach.

Visiting My Godson

Lost driving in my hometown on roads I thought I knew,
a rain-routed detour with powerlines down.
I'd been visiting my godson, who sat next to me at Rocco's,
kept putting his head on my shoulder, making
sure I was still there, said more than once he'd missed me.

Our routine, riding through the drive-through car wash,
each time newly amazed at the soap and thumping brushes,
he gets to put the quarters in the fat vacuums after,
pulls the pebbles from the floor mats as I paper towel
the windows for his inspection, nod of approval,
handshake of satisfaction. Then off to miniature golf
at Castlegate out on 57.

Driving home the long way, I hope
my tired old car holds out another hundred thousand miles—
nothing a little money, care and attention won't fix,
nothing a newer model can't improve.
It's all about time, timing belts, tune-ups,
having the proper mechanic,
knowing those ever-important back roads.

It is possible to get from Harmony to Belvidere
along Foul Rift on the river without ever having to hit
Route 519 if you know the right turns.
I have shown him this way and now there is no other.
We are agreed on how to go and where to get there.

Stillwater Summer

Victoria ate only ice cream, bought vanilla in bulk
each month when the check came. She'd scuttle
quickly away, gray ponytail swinging, if she saw me upstairs

but outside by the Chevy, doors open for air,
sunken into a tattered old lawn chair,
she'd talk to me sweetly and call for the cat.

Lorelei owned the house, latched the doors
or left them open on the nights I worked
swing shift, getting home after midnight,

when we'd watch TV together until very late.
Weekends, I'd move the furniture out of the way
so they could wax the wooden floors.

When I moved out in September, Lorelei kissed
both my cheeks and Victoria gave me a half-gallon
of ice cream, only vanilla, sweet none the less.

That was the last home I ever lived in,
though I've lived other places.

Last time I drove past, I saw a For Sale sign,
both cars still in the driveway, TV still flickering,
enjoying their ice-cream, but I didn't drop in.

Birdie

> *"but there were sorrows to be healed
> and mercy, mercy in this world."*
>   Jennifer Warnes, *Song of Bernadette*

After painting your room the color of sunshine,
we drove back from Oxford, spun out
on wet gravel coming down Hazen Road.

I over-corrected; we fish-tailed backwards,
you gripped both hands on the dash as we slid toward a ravine.
The rear wheel dipped over, you shot one steel-calm glance,

ready, reeling, perched on the edge. I slammed
the transmission to low drive, a second inch backwards,
dirt falling, we flushed out fifty swallows. We felt

the wheels grip, I gunned us back onto the road.

The name Bernadette means brave as a bear,
but we called you Birdie because you were fragile
although no one said so, least of all me. We shared

some kind of survival strengthened that day going
over the mountain, coming in useful through
your hospitalizations and my moving around.

Birds hide their symptoms better than most other creatures.
We painted your room the color of sunshine,
covered the darkness, we looked at each other rather

than down the abyss. Later, letters we wrote
as we flew in migration. You became Deryn
or Chelidon, my Branwyn. For years

I could find you by the wind and the water.
The day we ducked death, we flushed out fifty swallows—

you've flown that many years with them already,
the color of sunshine, remaining in flight.

Is home

A cylinder, ceramic, precarious above an earthen floor.
When the kitchen gods, in their random cleaning,
drop it, splinters will be found for years down the stairs,
round the bend, even in the den, throughout the large,

easy house. When bits or chunks have worked into
so many cracks and corners, is anything complete for this
moment, standing, where does it live? Were you in that
kitchen, balanced for fate, choosing to fall,

since the gods will not own you, although they may try
to dry you and return you to the rack. Once, Saraswati
made a clay heart and painted it real colors, held
it out the window, with pride, too excited to wait until

I got up to the studio to see it. Two beats in her hand,
alive, it jumped of its own will two stories down to shatter
on the sidewalk before me, reds not even dry, running
down through the gaps. Shards could not get back into

ground, though, nor could they be glued back into form.
Where do they really reside, these scattered, puzzled pieces?
In Jersey, Apollo sculpts birds. Once they are fired and firm,
he cements them to walls, grounded, rooted, never to journey

to Europe or Asia. How do they know where to stay?
Not a single one will ever fall in this lifetime. And not
a single one will fly. I just make them, says Apollo,
I don't promise them a thing. Perhaps someone will
pry one off, spirit it to Hong Kong, who knows?

I do. I know in my head but that's all. I move
earth into sand into glass into promise. I have
dropped my creations, like all careless artists. Rather
than sweep up what is left, I visit each sliver, each

character, where it lands, stay with it awhile, thinking
each of those outlying vistas with a single scrap
landed in dust, under carpet flap,
or between wall and floor,   is home.

D. Scott Humphries lives in northern New Jersey, where he was born and raised. He taught English abroad in Kassel, Germany and in Bangkok, Thailand from 2002 until 2016. The poems in *Finding Pahaquarra* were inspired by his return to the United States and to the Delaware River Valley after fourteen years away. These poems deal with issues of how one's personal history and identity are often intertwined with one's place, how we lose ourselves and our places through time and distance and how we find our way "home."

He currently teaches English at Sussex County Community College in Newton, New Jersey and is the Director of the Betty June Silconas Poetry Center as well as Editor of *The Stillwater Review*. He is also on the Board of Directors of the Luna Parc Atelier Foundation and is the creator of the Luna Parc Summer Poetry Nights in July reading series.

www.ingramcontent.com/pod-product-compliance
Lightning Source LLC
LaVergne TN
LVHW041600070426
835507LV00011B/1222